NEIL ARMSTRONG

WALKS ON THE MOON

By Nel Yomtov

Illustration By Samir Barrett and Dave Wheeler

Color By Gerardo Sandoval

BELLWETHER MEDIA • MINNEAPOLIS, MN

STRAY FROM REGULAR READS WITH BLACK SHEEP BOOKS. FEEL A RUSH WITH EVERY READ!

Library of Congress Cataloging-in-Publication Data

Yomtov, Nelson.
  Neil Armstrong Walks on the Moon / by Nel Yomtov.
    pages cm. -- (Black Sheep: Extraordinary Explorers)
  Summary: "Exciting illustrations follow the events of Neil Armstrong walking on the moon. The combination of brightly colored panels and leveled text is intended for students in grades 3 through 7"--Provided by publisher.
  Audience: Ages 7 to 12
  In graphic novel form.
  Includes bibliographical references and index.
  ISBN 978-1-62617-294-4 (hardcover: alk. paper)
  1. Project Apollo (U.S.)--Comic books, strips, etc. 2. Space flight to the moon--Comic books, strips, etc. 3. Armstrong, Neil, 1930-2012--Comic books, strips, etc. 4. Graphic novels. I. Title.
  TL789.8.U6A6823 2016
  629.45'4--dc23
                              2015006568

This edition first published in 2016 by Bellwether Media, Inc.

Printed in the United States of America, North Mankato, MN.

TABLE OF CONTENTS

Red text identifies
historical quotes.

The Race into Space

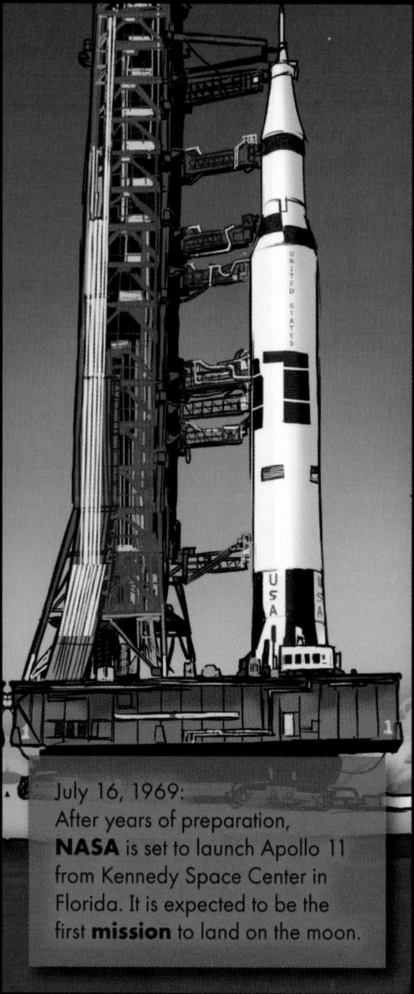

July 16, 1969:
After years of preparation, **NASA** is set to launch Apollo 11 from Kennedy Space Center in Florida. It is expected to be the first **mission** to land on the moon.

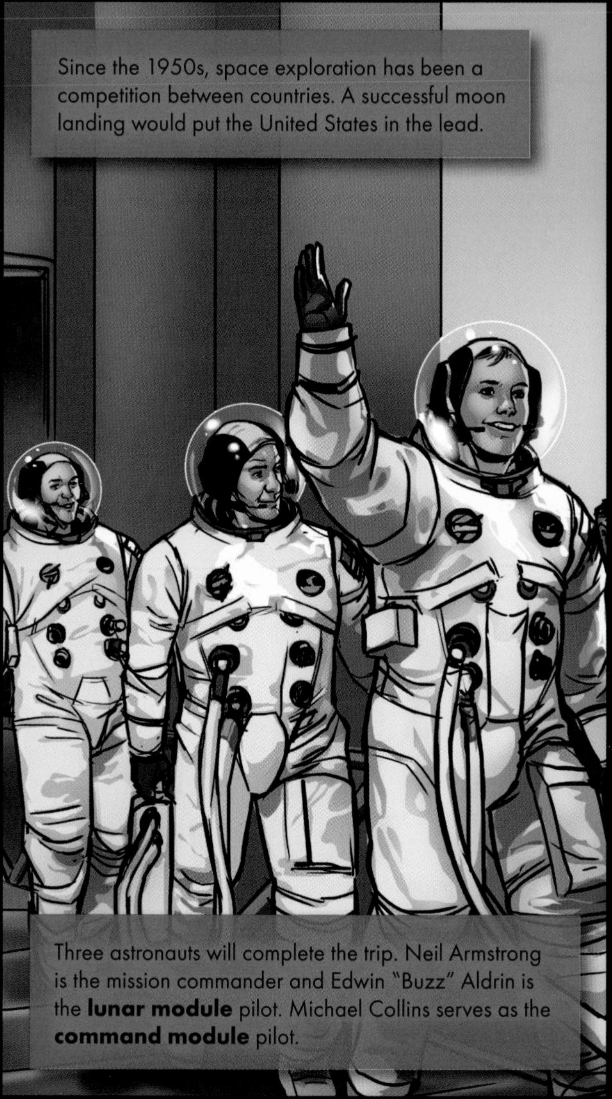

Since the 1950s, space exploration has been a competition between countries. A successful moon landing would put the United States in the lead.
Three astronauts will complete the trip. Neil Armstrong is the mission commander and Edwin "Buzz" Aldrin is the **lunar module** pilot. Michael Collins serves as the **command module** pilot.

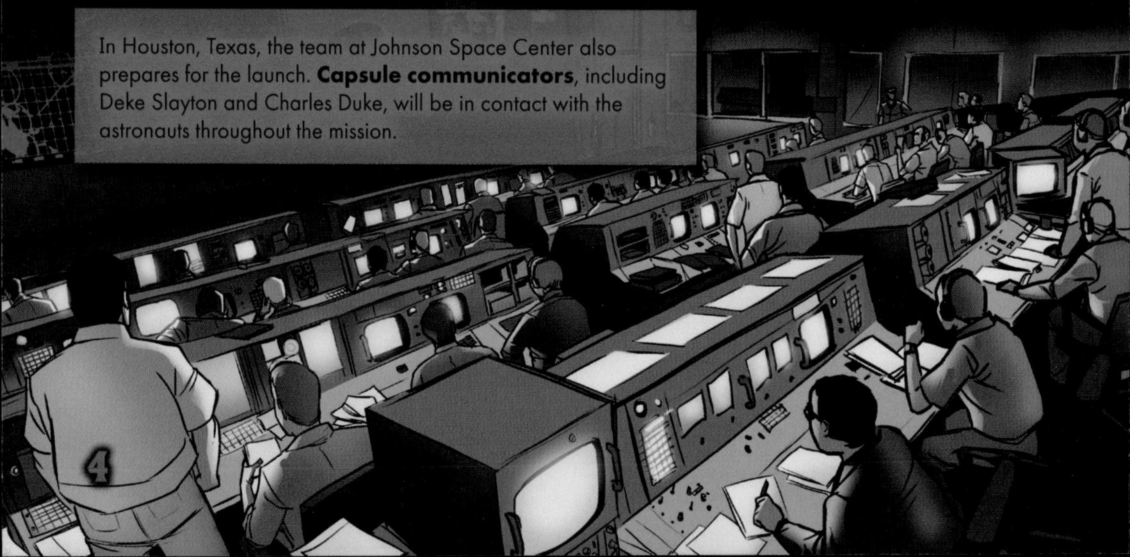

In Houston, Texas, the team at Johnson Space Center also prepares for the launch. **Capsule communicators**, including Deke Slayton and Charles Duke, will be in contact with the astronauts throughout the mission.

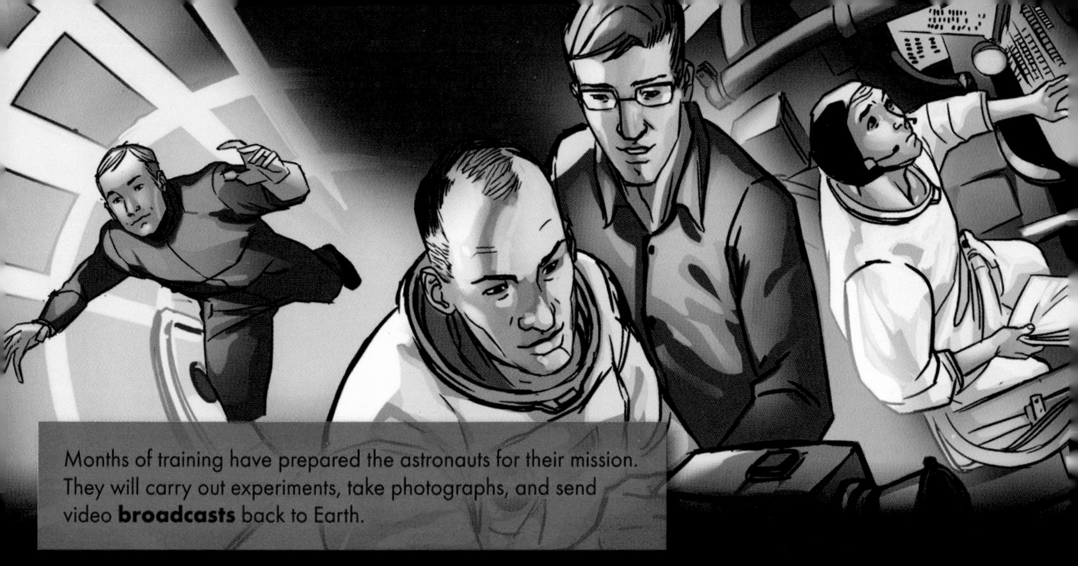
Months of training have prepared the astronauts for their mission. They will carry out experiments, take photographs, and send video **broadcasts** back to Earth.

The astronauts will fly up in *Columbia*. For much of the trip, they will live in *Columbia's* command module. The **service module** holds most of their fuel, oxygen, and water.

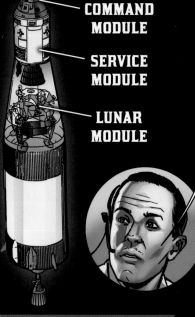

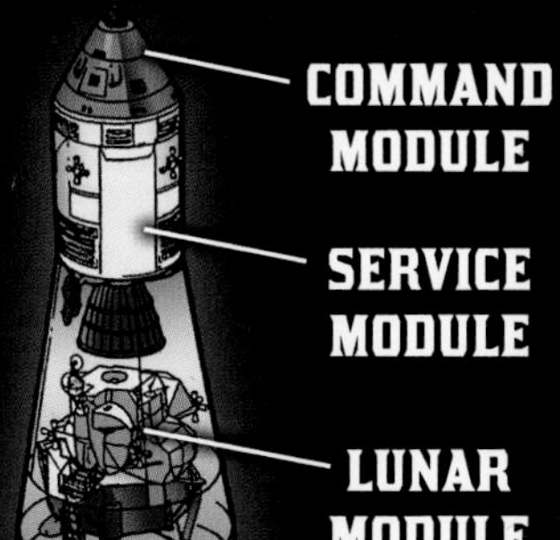
COMMAND MODULE
SERVICE MODULE
LUNAR MODULE

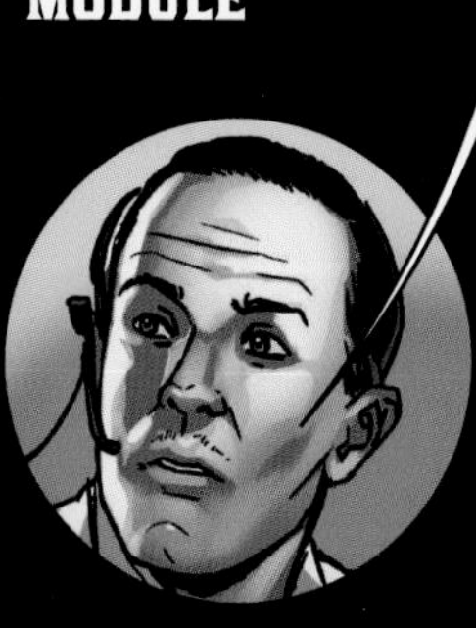

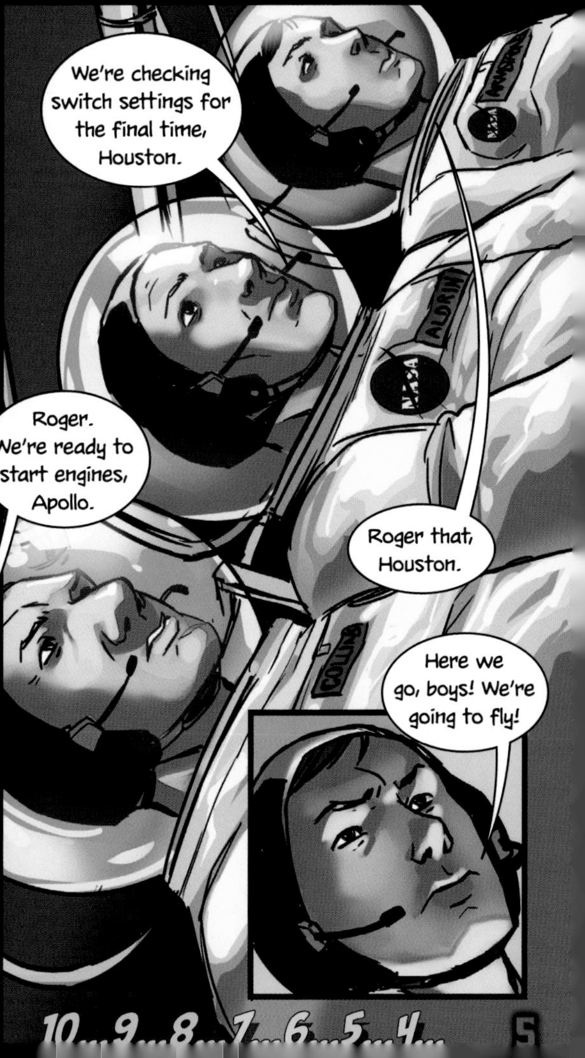
We're checking switch settings for the final time, Houston.
Roger. We're ready to start engines, Apollo.
Roger that, Houston.
Here we go, boys! We're going to fly!
10... 9... 8... 7... 6... 5... 4...

In space, the lunar module, *Eagle*, will separate from *Columbia*. While *Columbia* **orbits** the moon, *Eagle* will land on the moon's surface.

To the Moon!

9:32 a.m.
3...
2...
1...
LIFTOFF!
All engines running. Liftoff! We have a liftoff at 32 minutes past the hour. Liftoff on Apollo 11!
RROOAAARRRRRRR

Liftoff is smooth. You are looking good.
Roger. Hear you loud and clear, Houston.
After *Columbia* completes 1½ orbits of Earth, the crew fires an engine to escape the pull of Earth's **gravity**. They are on their way to the moon.
We have no complaints with any of the three stages on that ride. It was beautiful!
Get ready for separation, Apollo.
About 3½ hours after liftoff, it is time for one of the toughest steps of the mission. *Columbia* must **dock** with *Eagle*.
Columbia turns to meet *Eagle*. Then they dock.
SHHCLICK
That wasn't the smoothest docking I've ever done.
Well, it felt good from here.

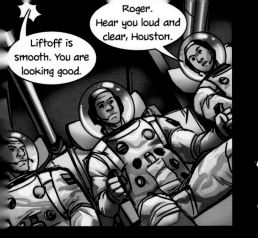

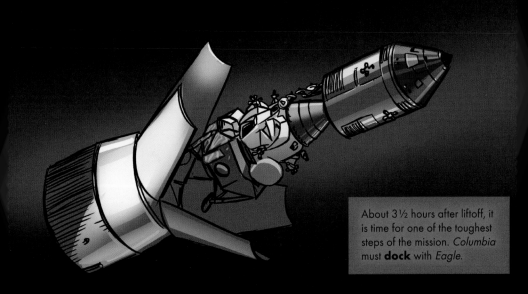

July 20, 1969:
After breakfast, Armstrong and Aldrin change their suits and move from *Columbia* into *Eagle*.

FWOOOSH

July 19, 1969:
Collins fires *Columbia's* rockets to slow the craft down as it begins orbiting the moon. The astronauts are now flying about 70 miles above the lunar surface.

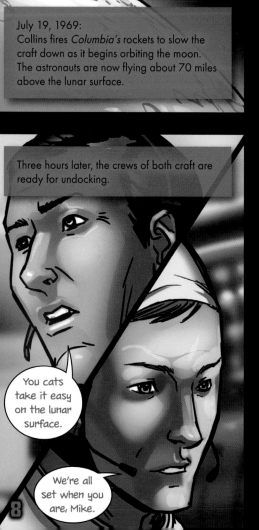

Three hours later, the crews of both craft are ready for undocking.

At just over 100 hours since liftoff, *Eagle* separates from *Columbia*. Collins will orbit the moon alone in *Columbia*.

You cats take it easy on the lunar surface.

We're all set when you are, Mike.

The *Eagle* has wings!

You've got a fine-looking flying machine there, *Eagle*!

8

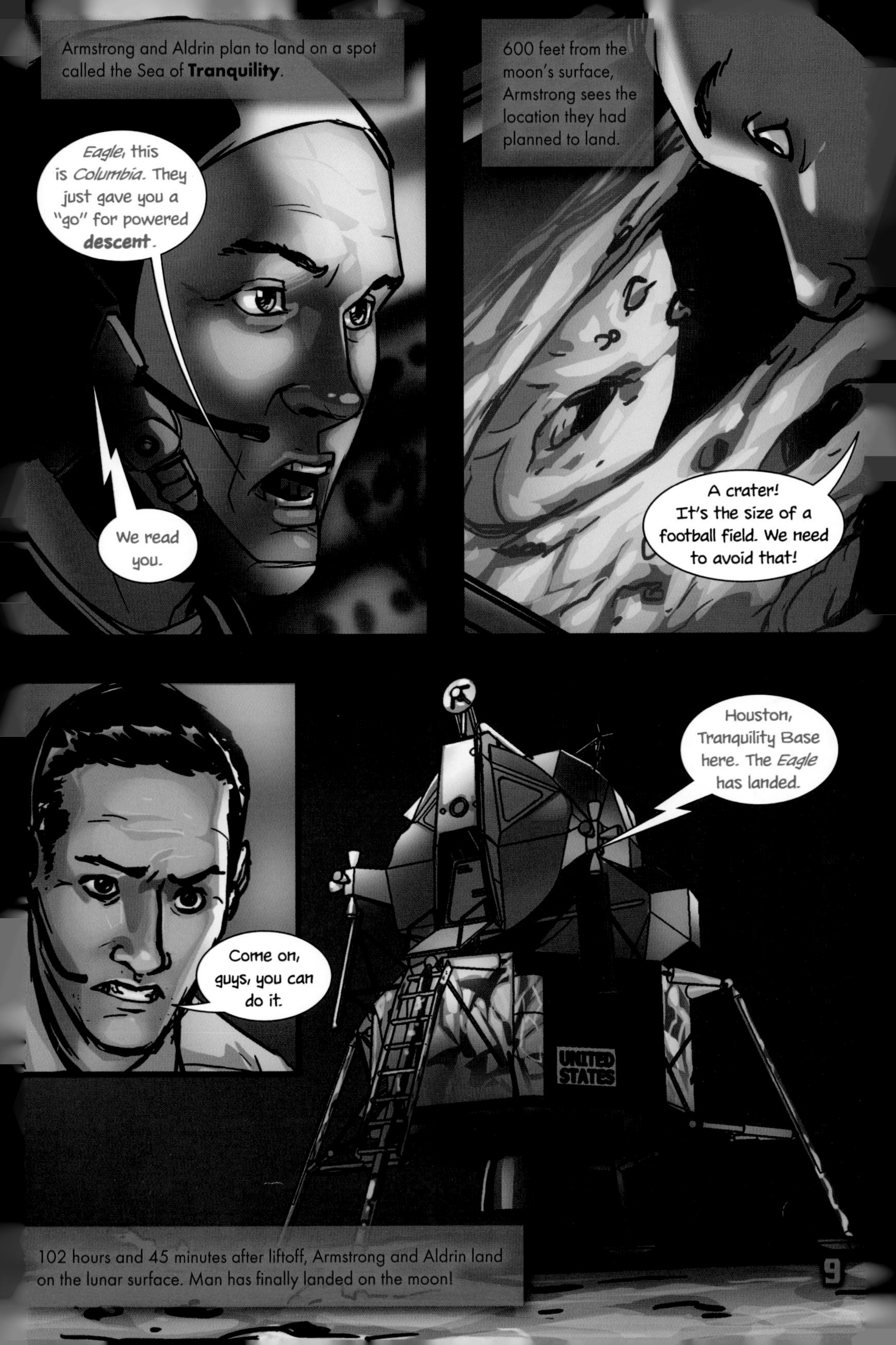
Armstrong and Aldrin plan to land on a spot called the Sea of **Tranquility**.
Eagle, this is *Columbia*. They just gave you a "go" for powered **descent**.
We read you.
600 feet from the moon's surface, Armstrong sees the location they had planned to land.
A crater! It's the size of a football field. We need to avoid that!
Come on, guys, you can do it.
Houston, Tranquility Base here. The *Eagle* has landed.
UNITED STATES
102 hours and 45 minutes after liftoff, Armstrong and Aldrin land on the lunar surface. Man has finally landed on the moon!

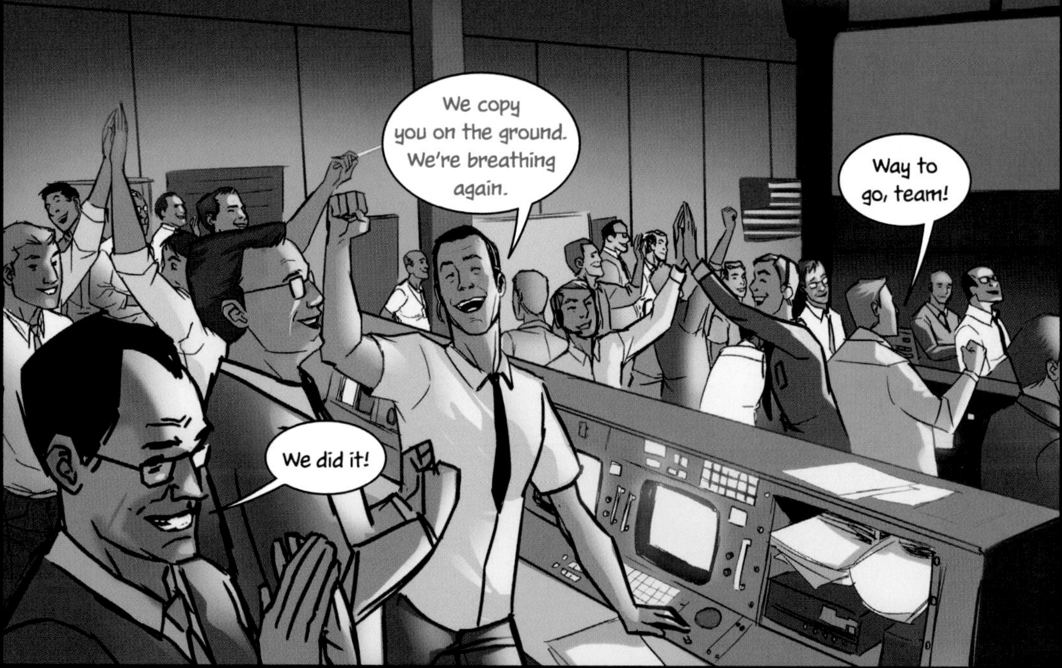
We copy you on the ground. We're breathing again.
Way to go, team!
We did it!

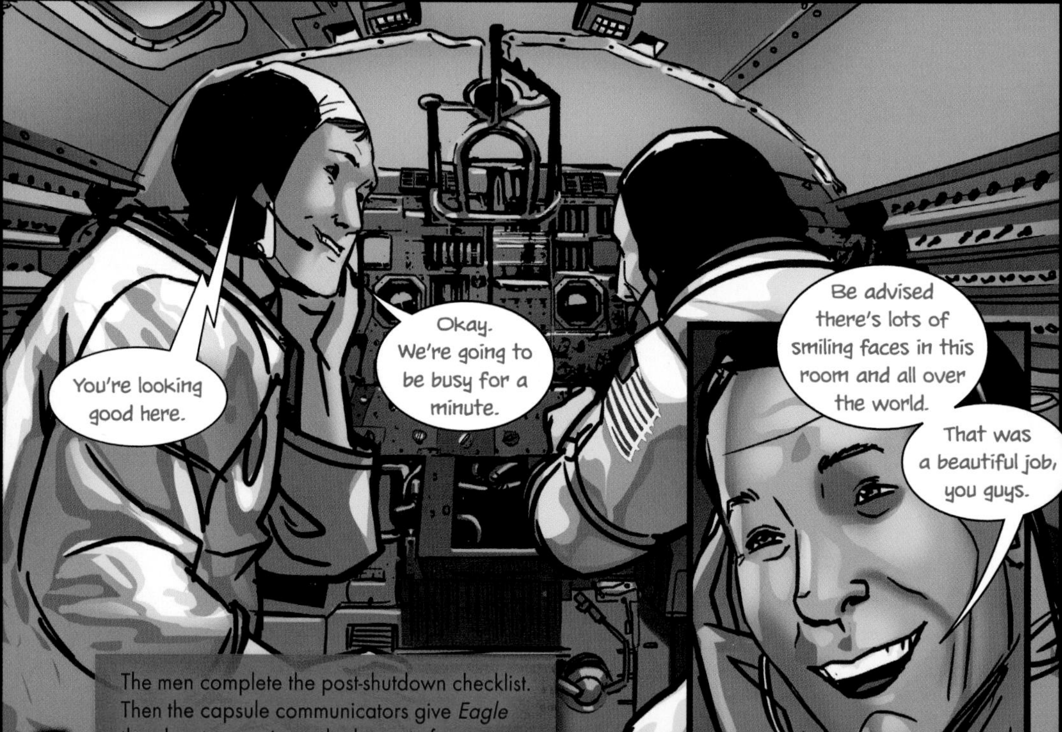
You're looking good here.
Okay. We're going to be busy for a minute.
Be advised there's lots of smiling faces in this room and all over the world.
That was a beautiful job, you guys.
The men complete the post-shutdown checklist. Then the capsule communicators give *Eagle* the okay to remain on the lunar surface.

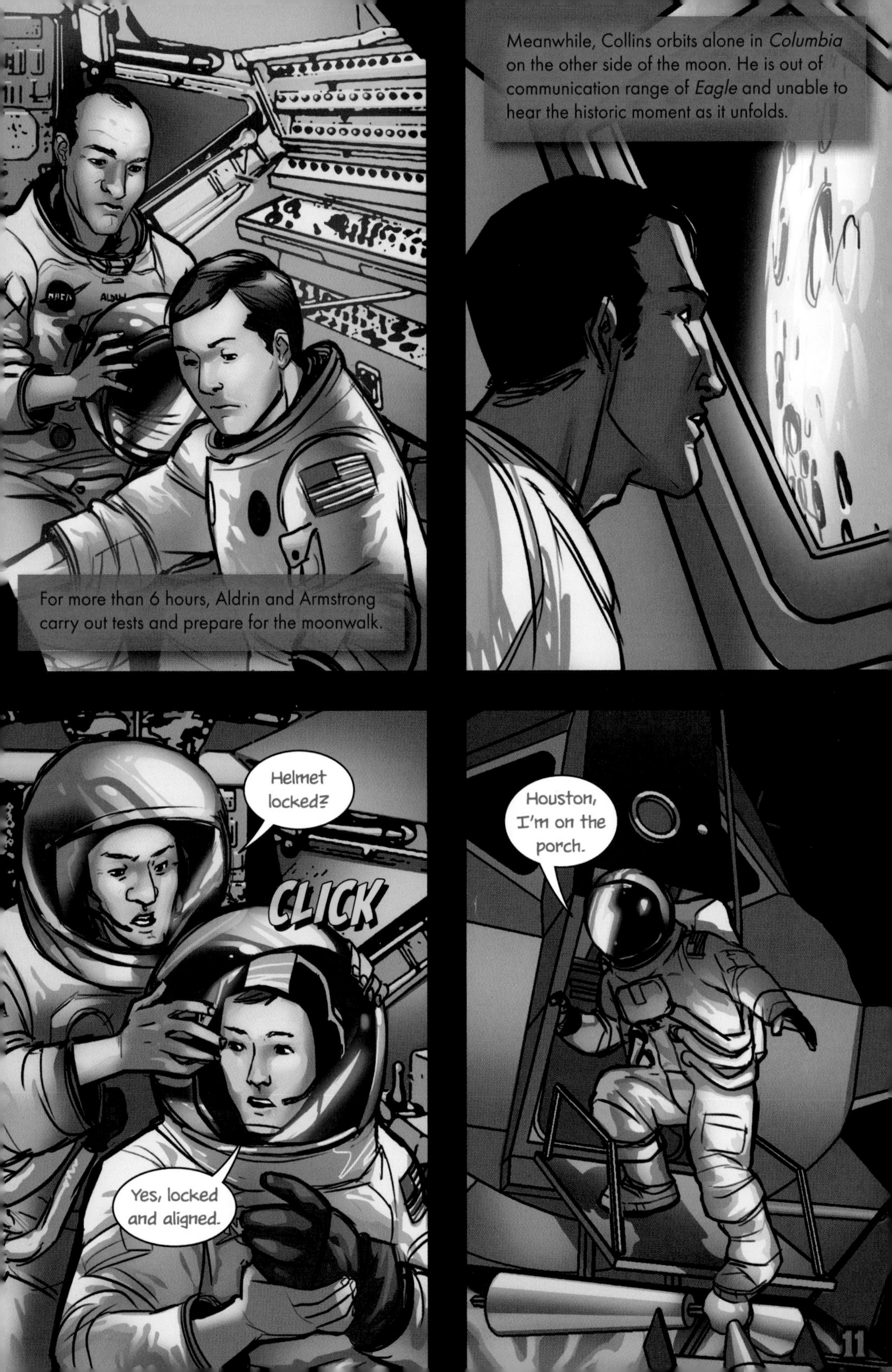
For more than 6 hours, Aldrin and Armstrong carry out tests and prepare for the moonwalk.
Meanwhile, Collins orbits alone in *Columbia* on the other side of the moon. He is out of communication range of *Eagle* and unable to hear the historic moment as it unfolds.
Helmet locked?
CLICK
Yes, locked and aligned.
Houston, I'm on the porch.

"One Giant Leap for Mankind"

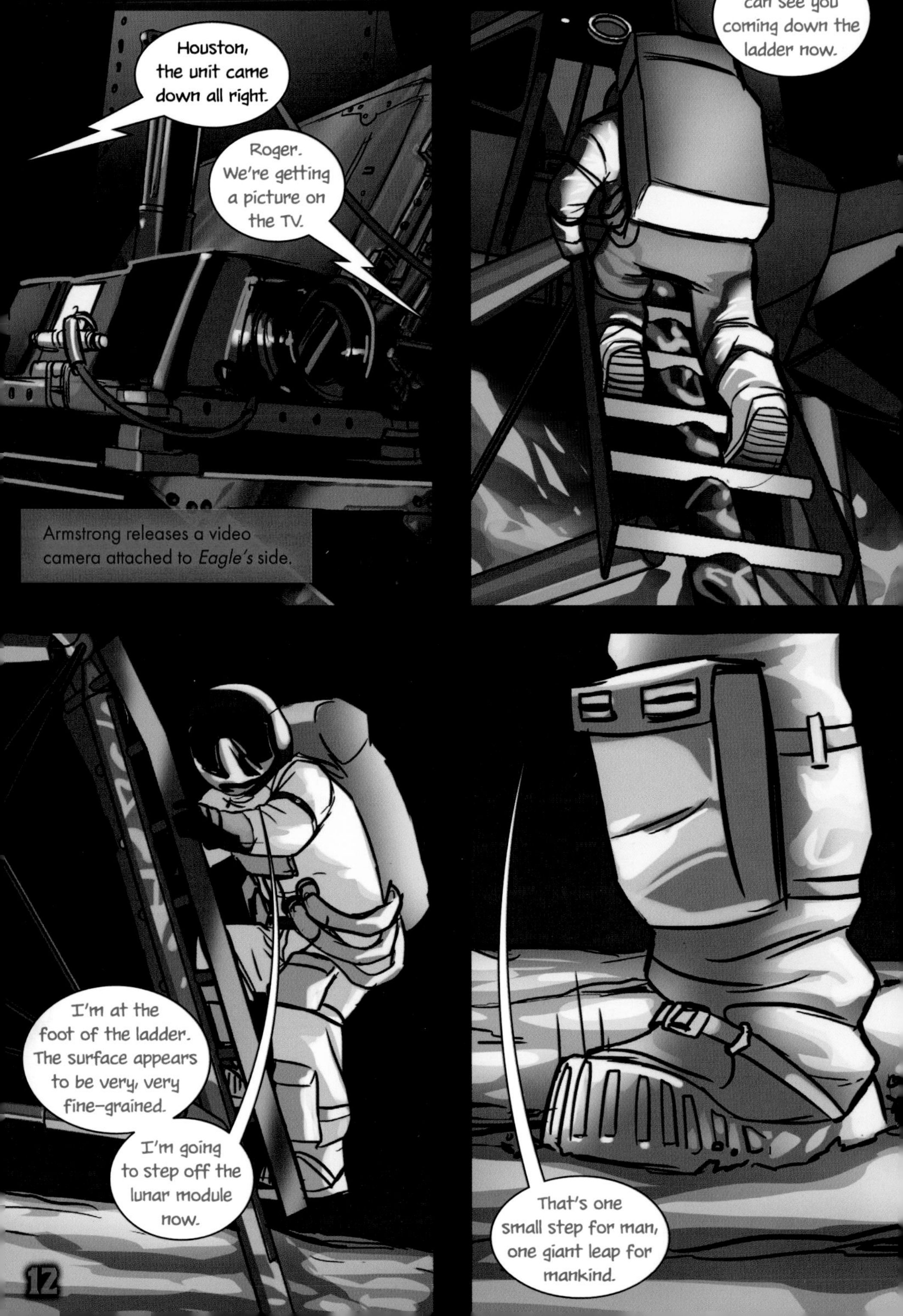
Houston, the unit came down all right.
Roger. We're getting a picture on the TV.
Armstrong releases a video camera attached to *Eagle's* side.
Neil, we can see you coming down the ladder now.
I'm at the foot of the ladder. The surface appears to be very, very fine-grained.
I'm going to step off the lunar module now.
That's one small step for man, one giant leap for mankind.

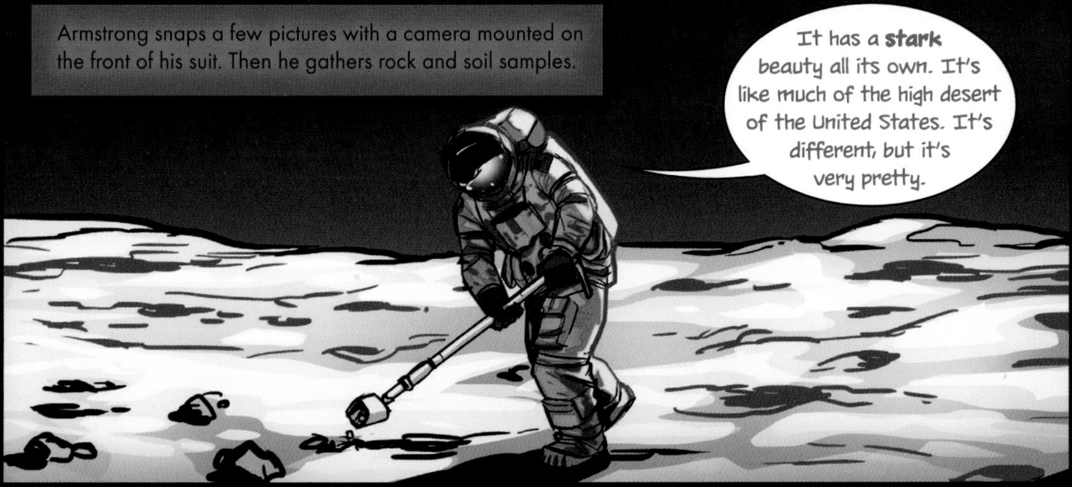
Armstrong snaps a few pictures with a camera mounted on the front of his suit. Then he gathers rock and soil samples.
It has a **stark** beauty all its own. It's like much of the high desert of the United States. It's different, but it's very pretty.

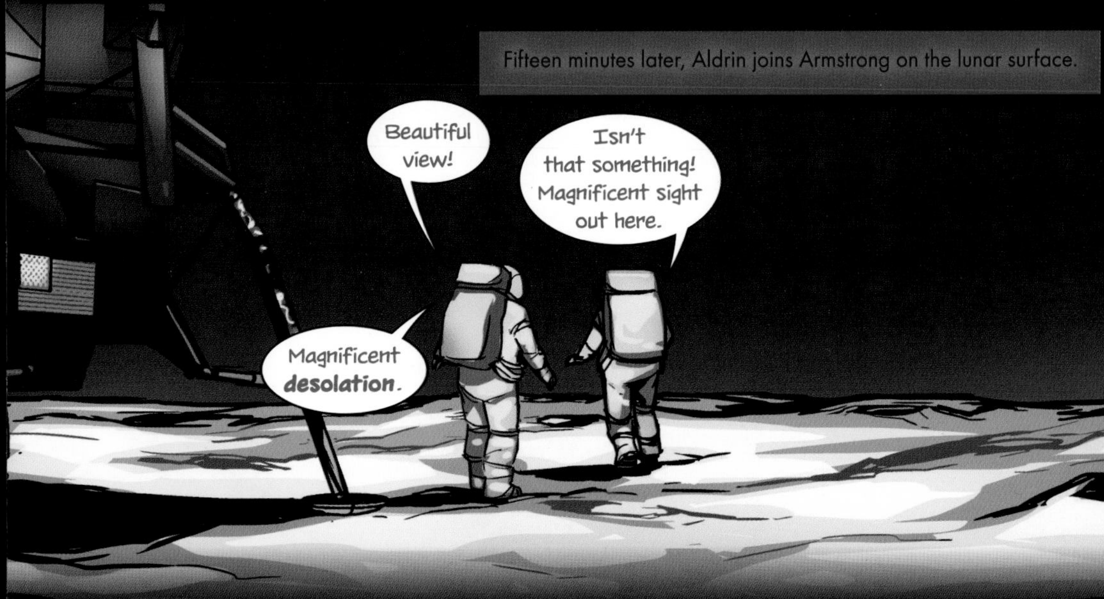
Fifteen minutes later, Aldrin joins Armstrong on the lunar surface.
Beautiful view!
Isn't that something! Magnificent sight out here.
Magnificent **desolation**.

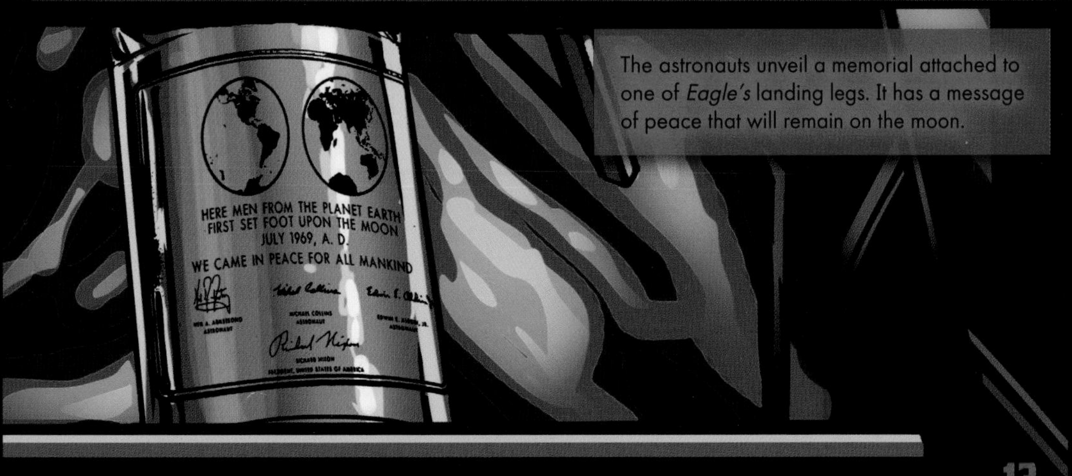
The astronauts unveil a memorial attached to one of *Eagle's* landing legs. It has a message of peace that will remain on the moon.
HERE MEN FROM THE PLANET EARTH FIRST SET FOOT UPON THE MOON JULY 1969, A.D.
WE CAME IN PEACE FOR ALL MANKIND

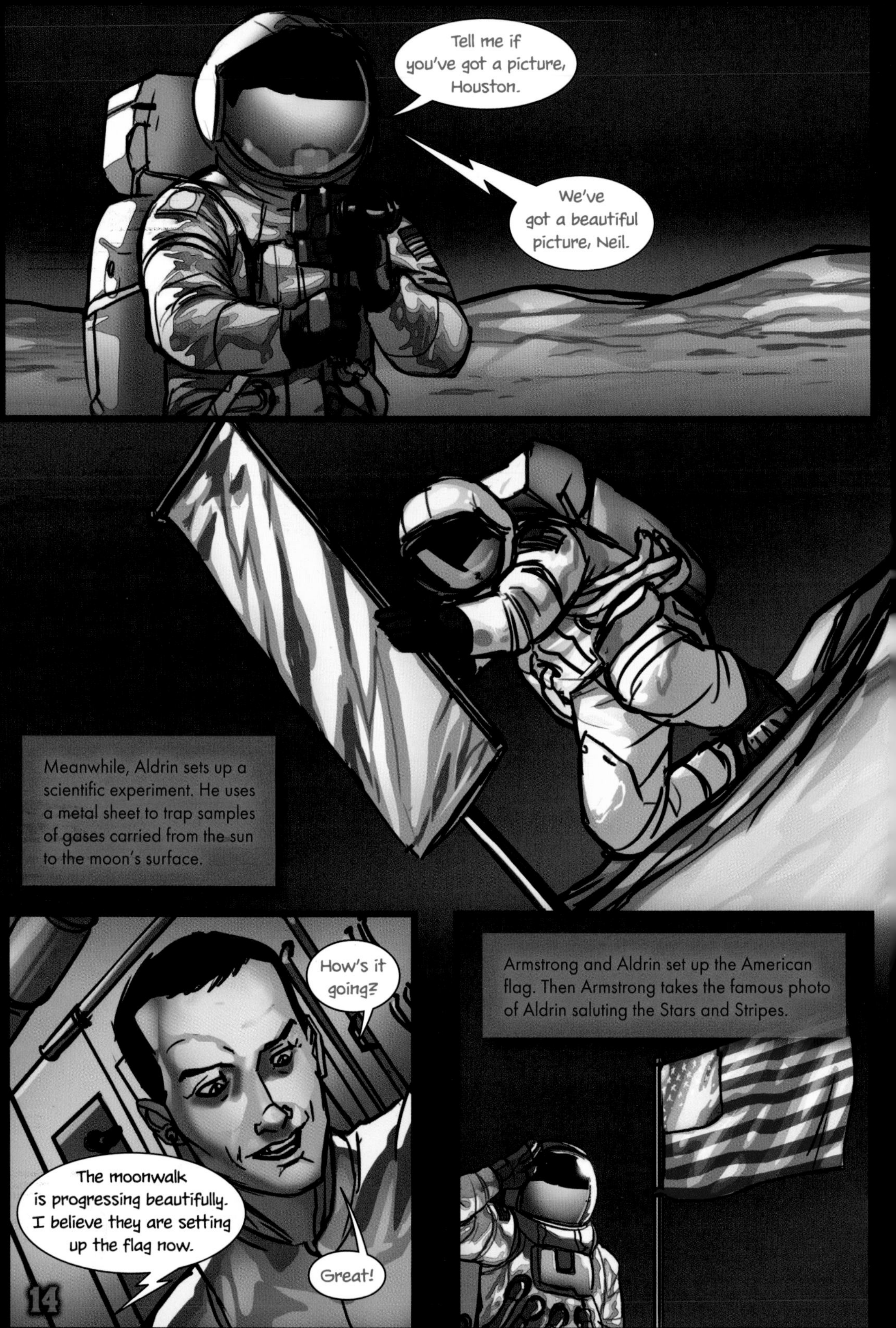
Tell me if you've got a picture, Houston.
We've got a beautiful picture, Neil.
Meanwhile, Aldrin sets up a scientific experiment. He uses a metal sheet to trap samples of gases carried from the sun to the moon's surface.
How's it going?
The moonwalk is progressing beautifully. I believe they are setting up the flag now.
Great!
Armstrong and Aldrin set up the American flag. Then Armstrong takes the famous photo of Aldrin saluting the Stars and Stripes.

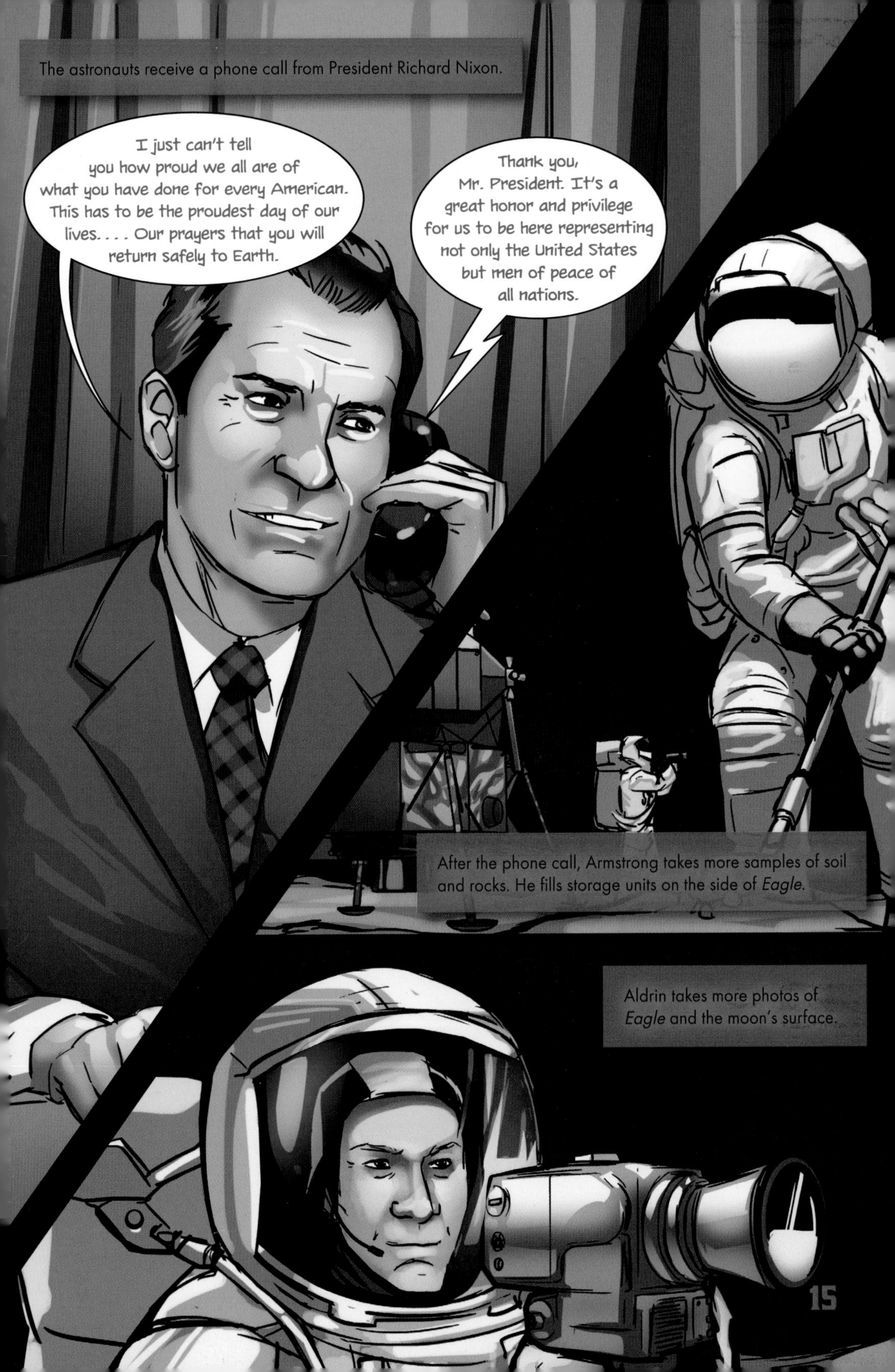

The astronauts receive a phone call from President Richard Nixon.
I just can't tell you how proud we all are of what you have done for every American. This has to be the proudest day of our lives. . . . Our prayers that you will return safely to Earth.
Thank you, Mr. President. It's a great honor and privilege for us to be here representing not only the United States but men of peace of all nations.
After the phone call, Armstrong takes more samples of soil and rocks. He fills storage units on the side of *Eagle*.
Aldrin takes more photos of *Eagle* and the moon's surface.

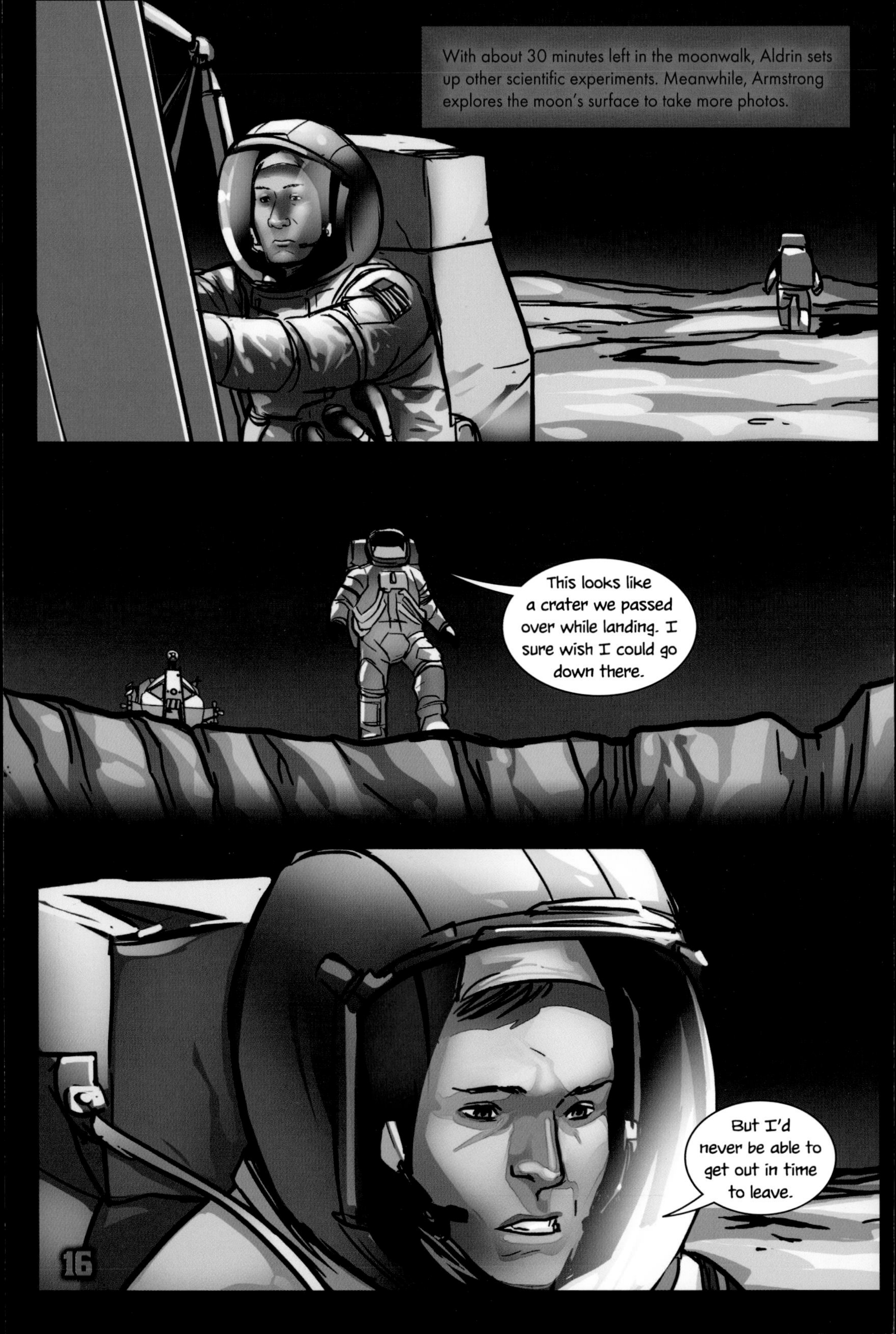
With about 30 minutes left in the moonwalk, Aldrin sets up other scientific experiments. Meanwhile, Armstrong explores the moon's surface to take more photos.
This looks like a crater we passed over while landing. I sure wish I could go down there.
But I'd never be able to get out in time to leave.

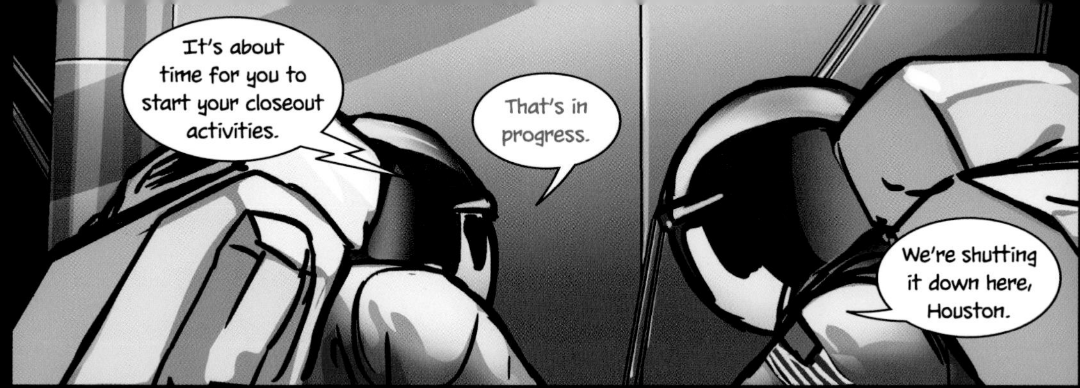
It's about time for you to start your closeout activities.
That's in progress.
We're shutting it down here, Houston.

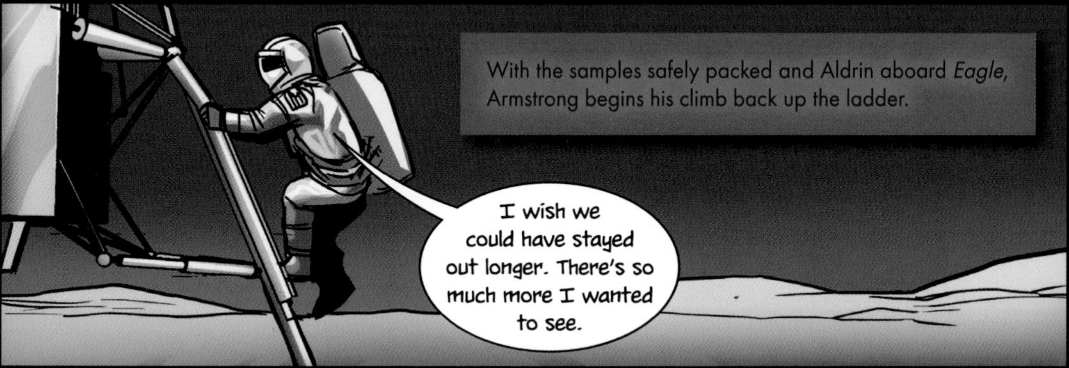
With the samples safely packed and Aldrin aboard *Eagle*, Armstrong begins his climb back up the ladder.
I wish we could have stayed out longer. There's so much more I wanted to see.

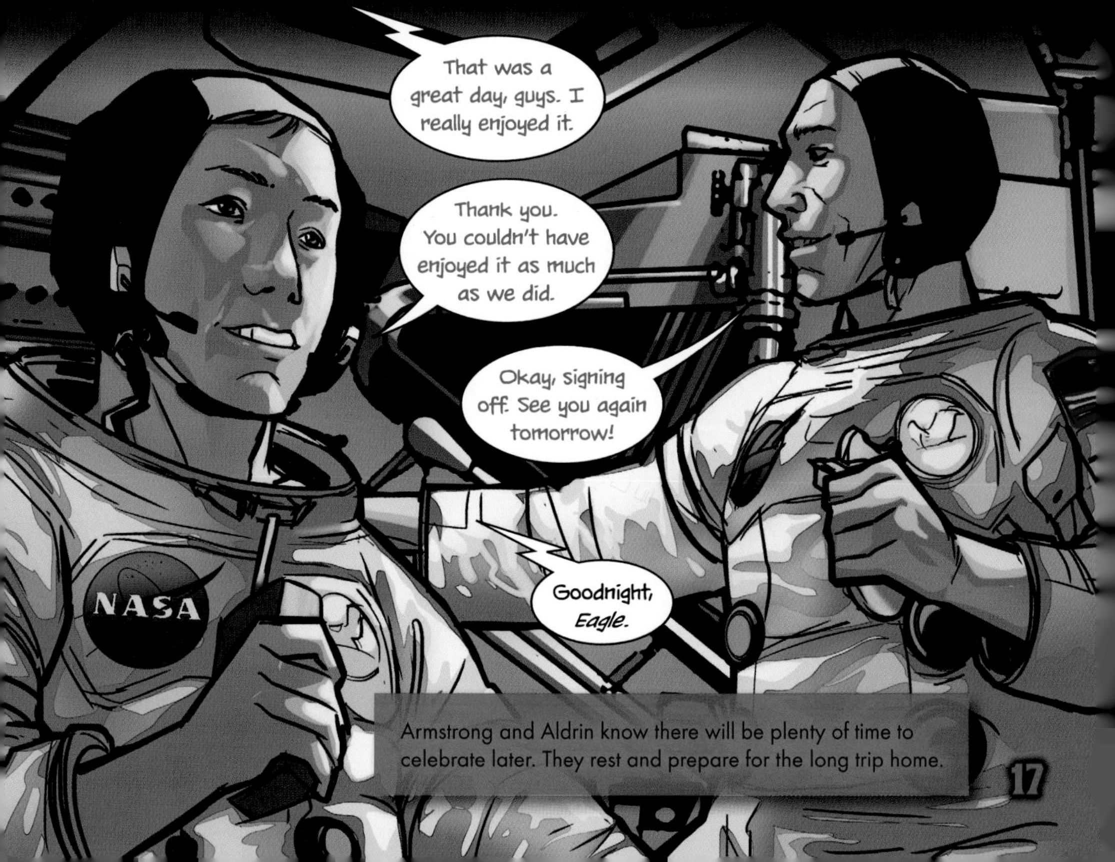
That was a great day, guys. I really enjoyed it.
Thank you. You couldn't have enjoyed it as much as we did.
Okay, signing off. See you again tomorrow!
Goodnight, *Eagle*.
NASA
Armstrong and Aldrin know there will be plenty of time to celebrate later. They rest and prepare for the long trip home.

GOING HOME

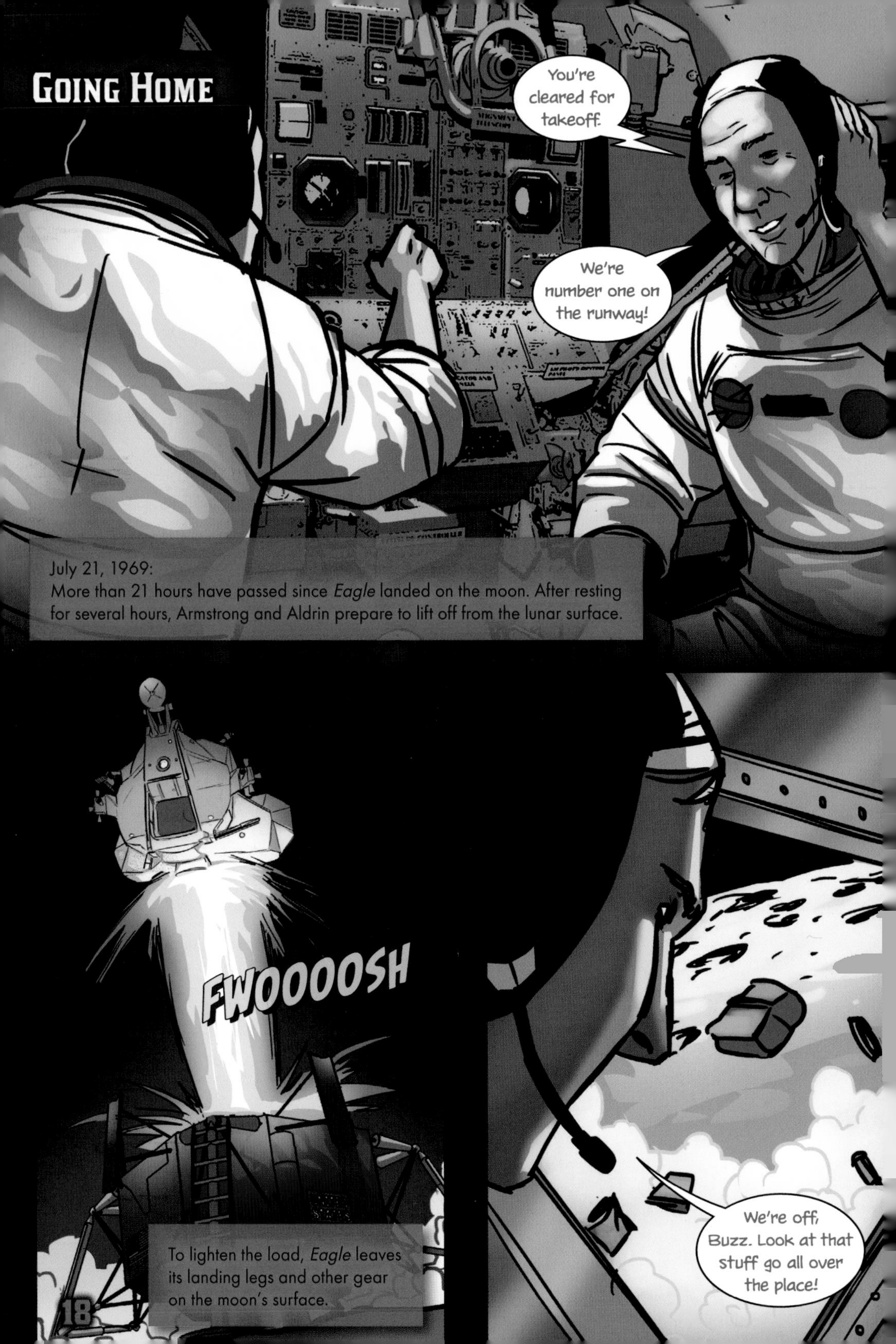
You're cleared for takeoff.
We're number one on the runway!
July 21, 1969:
More than 21 hours have passed since *Eagle* landed on the moon. After resting for several hours, Armstrong and Aldrin prepare to lift off from the lunar surface.
FWOOOOSH
To lighten the load, *Eagle* leaves its landing legs and other gear on the moon's surface.
We're off, Buzz. Look at that stuff go all over the place!

Columbia has orbited the moon 27 times since undocking from Eagle.

The Eagle is back in orbit!

There they are!

Four hours after leaving the moon's surface, Eagle prepares to dock with Columbia.

Minutes later, Armstrong and Aldrin leave Eagle and enter Columbia. They reunite with Collins and unload their samples from the moon.

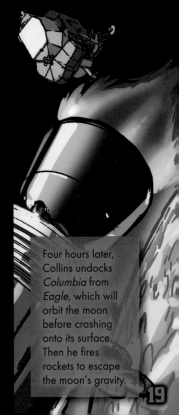

Four hours later, Collins undocks Columbia from Eagle, which will orbit the moon before crashing onto its surface. Then he fires rockets to escape the moon's gravity.

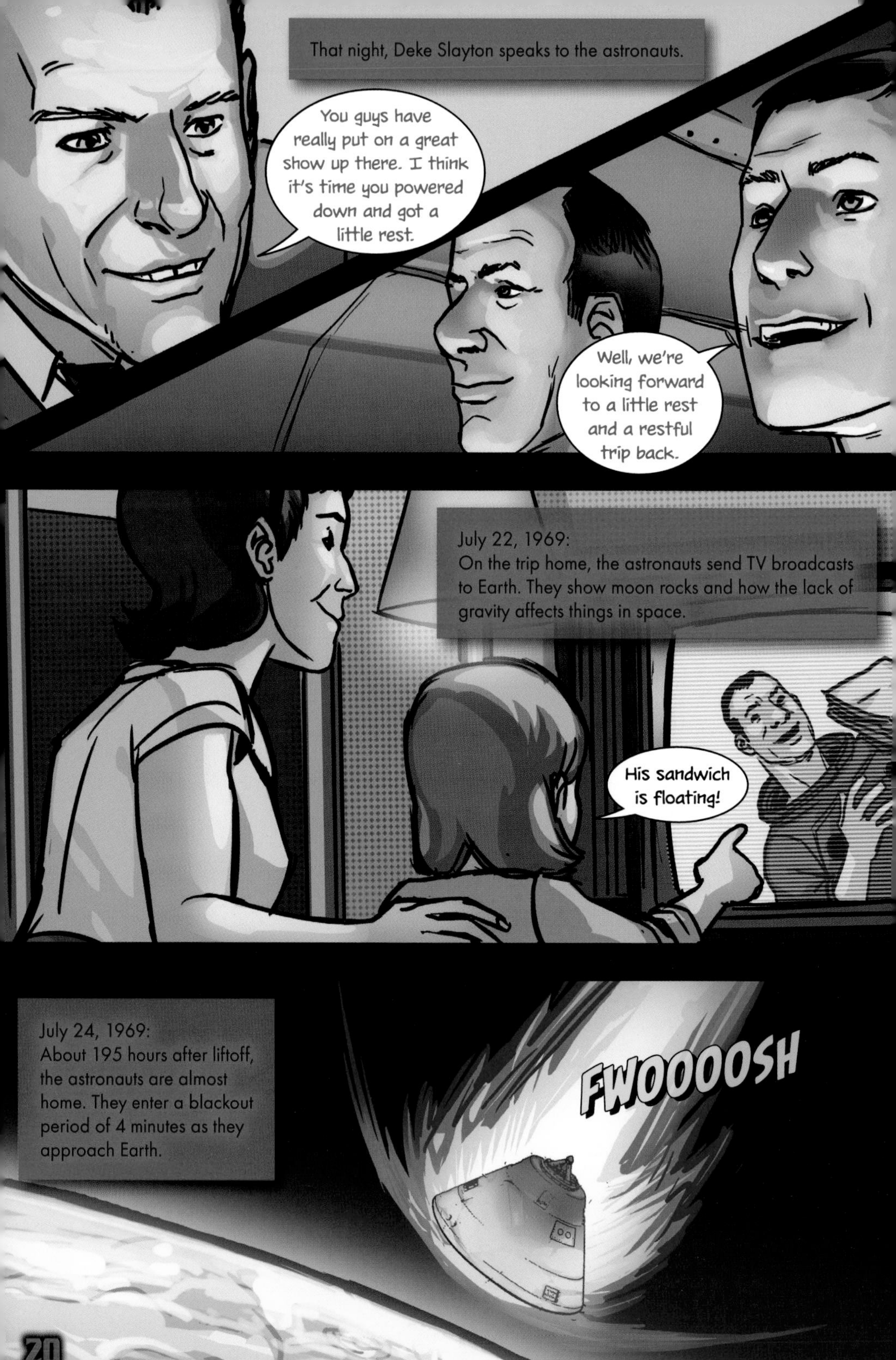
That night, Deke Slayton speaks to the astronauts.
You guys have really put on a great show up there. I think it's time you powered down and got a little rest.
Well, we're looking forward to a little rest and a restful trip back.
July 22, 1969:
On the trip home, the astronauts send TV broadcasts to Earth. They show moon rocks and how the lack of gravity affects things in space.
His sandwich is floating!
July 24, 1969:
About 195 hours after liftoff, the astronauts are almost home. They enter a blackout period of 4 minutes as they approach Earth.
FWOOOOSH

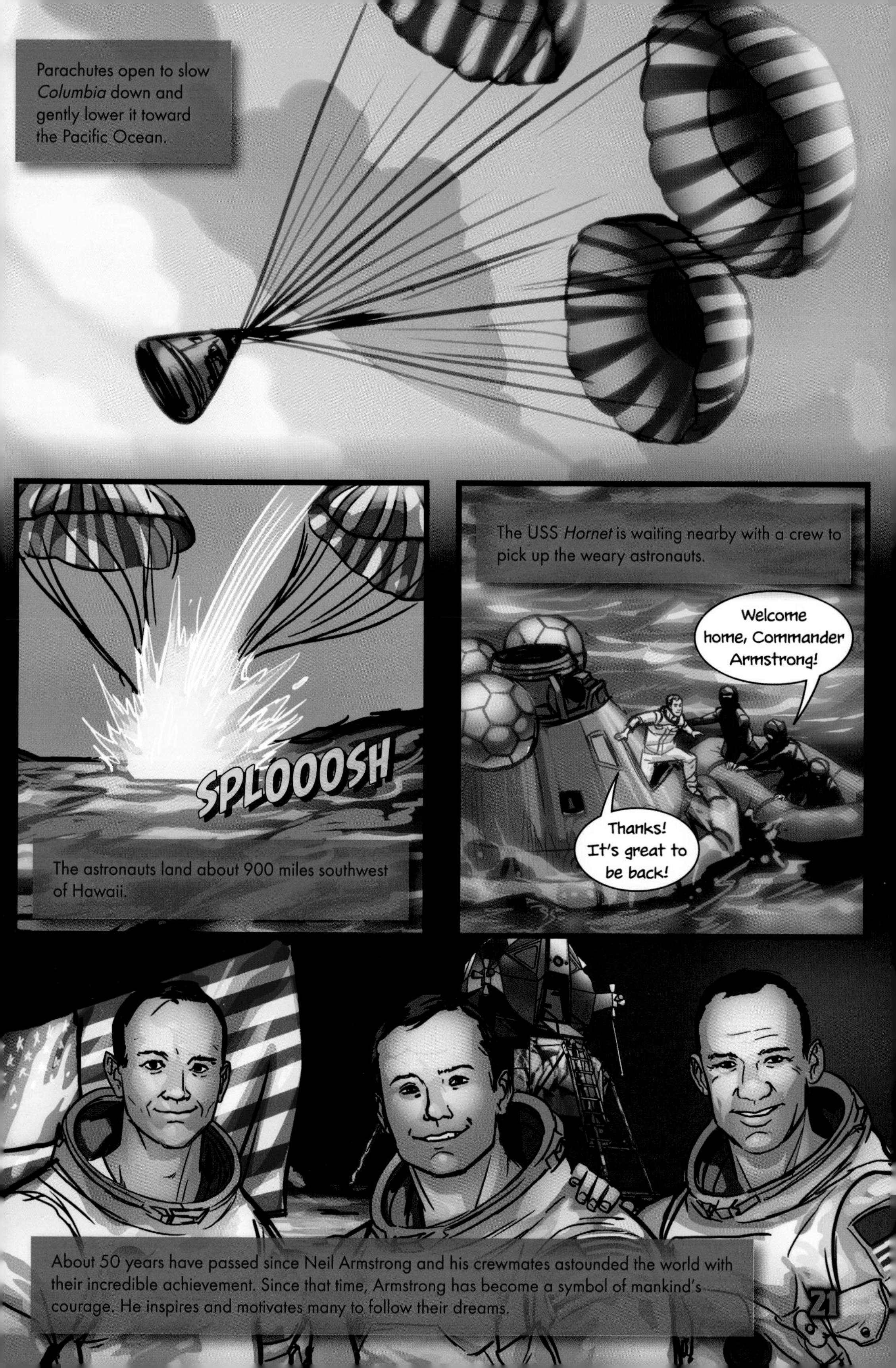
Parachutes open to slow *Columbia* down and gently lower it toward the Pacific Ocean.
SPLOOOSH
The astronauts land about 900 miles southwest of Hawaii.
The USS *Hornet* is waiting nearby with a crew to pick up the weary astronauts.
Welcome home, Commander Armstrong!
Thanks! It's great to be back!
About 50 years have passed since Neil Armstrong and his crewmates astounded the world with their incredible achievement. Since that time, Armstrong has become a symbol of mankind's courage. He inspires and motivates many to follow their dreams.

MORE ABOUT ARMSTRONG AND APOLLO 11

- After the Apollo 11 mission, Neil Armstrong continued to work in research and technology for NASA.

- Throughout the trip, Apollo 11 traveled a total of 953,054 miles (1,533,792 kilometers).

- One of the first things Armstrong did on the moon was take rock samples. He did this in case the mission ran into trouble and he had to stop the moonwalk early.

- Armstrong and Aldrin brought back about 48 pounds (22 kilograms) of rocks and soil from the moon.

- In addition to the memorial and the American flag, the astronauts also left an Apollo 1 mission patch, an olive branch, and messages of peace from the leaders of 73 countries.

- About 600 million people around the world watched the moon landing on the television broadcast.

Glossary

broadcasts—television signals sent all over the world

capsule communicators—teams of NASA employees that were in contact with the astronauts

command module—the part of an Apollo spacecraft that served as the control center for the spacecraft

descent—a downward movement

desolation—being empty or lonely

dock—to connect spacecraft together while in space

gravity—the force that pulls objects towards each other

lunar module—the part of an Apollo spacecraft that landed on the moon's surface

mission—an important task or assignment

NASA—short for National Aeronautics and Space Administration; NASA is the agency that oversees U.S. space exploration.

orbits—moves in a circular path around a planet or moon in space

service module—the part of an Apollo spacecraft that carried supplies and equipment for the mission

stark—being bare or empty

tranquility—being quiet and peaceful; the Apollo 11 crew landed in the moon's Sea of Tranquility.

To Learn More

AT THE LIBRARY

Adamson, Thomas K. *The First Moon Landing*. Mankato, Minn.: Capstone, 2007.

Stone, Adam. *The Apollo 13 Mission*. Minneapolis, Minn.: Bellwether Media, 2014.

Yomtov, Nel. *The Apollo 11 Moon Landing*. Chicago, Ill.: Heinemann Library, 2014.

ON THE WEB

Learning more about Neil Armstrong is as easy as 1, 2, 3.

1. Go to www.factsurfer.com.
2. Enter "Neil Armstrong" into the search box.
3. Click the "Surf" button and you will see a list of related web sites.

With factsurfer.com, finding more information is just a click away.

Index